Endorsements

Using words to make images that recall lived experience--this is poetry at its best. The poet adds comments that cause us to reflect and quotations from the world's sages that set the whole in our shared intellectual history. Fundamental transformation is the result. This indeed is life and poetry at its best. James E. Royster, Ph.D., *Have This Mind: Supreme Happiness, Ultimate Realization, and the Four Great Religions--An Integral Adventure.*

The author is a "Monarch of Poetry" writing from her life's experience of 25 adventurous years of spiritual recovery. Her metamorphosis is the music of recovery. As I read the book I marveled at her lyrics and its summation of creation wherein "all is good." Howard I. Westin, *teacher and lecturer of the Historical Jesus and A Course in Miracles.*

The poems on these pages are powerful and a must read for anyone associated with an alcoholic personality or connected with anyone in non-recovery. The book is a triumph in recovery, forgiveness and healing. It offers a way to take control of your life, let go of the past and live in the present. You can't read these poems without shedding a tear or two.

Mary Westcott begins her book by making me remember my childhood with all the unique joys, sorrows, sounds, smells and feelings of growing up. She will take you there, too. Then she catapults you beyond, churning all the emotions of loss and grieving, finally arriving at acceptance, gratitude and peace. So many of her insights are universal and a beacon for the reader to identify with the poems, affirmations and lessons. As I arrived at the end, I wanted to plant a butterfly bush, swim in the ocean or just rejoice. In Mary's words, "There must be dark in order to come into the light." *Linda A. terBurg, Author "How to Sell Your Books: Marketing Workbook."*

Also by Mary L. Westcott

Brain Custody, Argonne Hotel Press, December 1999
Fishing for Light, Argonne Hotel Press, April 2002
Lopsided Love, Argonne Hotel Press, September 2004
Greedy for Steeples and Stars, Amazon Kindle and Kindle Direct
      Publishing, January 17, 2013
Dangling Retina of a Moon, Amazon Kindle and Kindle Direct
      Publishing, January 23, 2013

Fluttering on Earth

A Journey of Healing and Recovery through Poetry

POEMS BY:

Mary L. Westcott

BALBOA
PRESS

A DIVISION OF HAY HOUSE

Balboa Press books may be ordered through booksellers or by contacting:

Balboa Press
A Division of Hay House
1663 Liberty Drive
Bloomington, IN 47403
www.balboapress.com
1 (877) 407-4847

Because of the dynamic nature of the Internet, any web addresses or links contained in this book may have changed since publication and may no longer be valid. The views expressed in this work are solely those of the author and do not necessarily reflect the views of the publisher, and the publisher hereby disclaims any responsibility for them.

The author of this book does not dispense medical advice or prescribe the use of any technique as a form of treatment for physical, emotional, or medical problems without the advice of a physician, either directly or indirectly. The intent of the author is only to offer information of a general nature to help you in your quest for emotional and spiritual well-being. In the event you use any of the information in this book for yourself, which is your constitutional right, the author and the publisher assume no responsibility for your actions.

Any people depicted in stock imagery provided by Thinkstock are models, and such images are being used for illustrative purposes only.
Certain stock imagery © Thinkstock.

Print information available on the last page.

ISBN: 978-1-5043-2820-3 (sc)
ISBN: 978-1-5043-2822-7 (hc)
ISBN: 978-1-5043-2821-0 (e)

Library of Congress Control Number: 2015902588

Balboa Press rev. date: 03/11/2015

This book is dedicated to all those in recovery programs such as Alcoholics Anonymous and Al Anon and to those who have struggled with relationships with alcoholics.

"Once upon a time, I dreamt I was a butterfly, fluttering hither and thither, to all intents and purposes a butterfly. I was conscious only of my happiness as a butterfly, unaware that I was myself. Soon I awaked, and there I was, veritably myself again. Now I do not know whether I was then a man dreaming I was a butterfly, or whether I am now a butterfly, dreaming I am a man."
Chuang-Tzu

Preface

This collection of poetry originated many years ago when I wrote about my experiences and my relationships with several active alcoholics. I use the image of the butterfly because these creatures are among the most beautiful in the world, and I attach spiritual significance to them. In Aztec folklore, butterflies are said to be the reincarnation of warriors. The Japanese consider the butterfly to be the personification of a person's soul; whether they are living, dying, or already dead. One Japanese superstition says that if a butterfly enters your guestroom and alights behind a bamboo screen, the person whom you most love is coming to see you. In some older cultures, butterflies symbolize rebirth after being inside a cocoon for a period of time. In poetry, they often represent freedom, whimsy, or transformation.

I started writing poetry about 25 years ago when I wanted an avocation other than my career in public health. Since that time I have undergone a spiritual change through twelve step programs, Unity teachings, A Course in Miracles, meditation, and writing. The metamorphosis and the poems that accompanied this change are chronicled here.

By letting go of grievances, forgiving those who I feel have wronged me, finding beauty in nature, and feeling grateful for my many blessings, I have become a person who is unknown to my former self. For that I am grateful.

The format of the collection consists of a poem on one page and an affirmation with a statement about the poem on the page following in order to enhance understanding of the poem. I have found that affirmations are useful tools for turning around negative thoughts. The poems are arranged in order from darker themes to lighter, more spiritual themes. These poems and accompanying affirmations are inspirational and can help others overcome the difficulty of a relationship with a non-recovering alcoholic or other addicted person. There are many paths to recovery that offer hope for dealing with the toughest and most traumatic of relationships. This is one of those paths.

Acknowledgements

I wish to thank Albert deSilver for providing the vehicle for many of the later poems at both Esalen Institute and Omega Institute in his Meditation and Writing classes. I'd also like to acknowledge the comments of Angela Love and Linda terBerg from the Unity of the Villages Writing group—thanks for your laughter and astute critiquing of my poems. In addition, the year-long writing group I participated in through the Unitarian Universalist Fellowship of Marion County was very helpful in providing the germ of many of the later poems—gratitude goes to Peggy Miller and Bernie Greenberg, in particular. Howard Westin, a teacher extraordinaire of "A Course in Miracles," is greatly appreciated for his encouragement and support. I also want to thank my niece, Charlotte F. Westcott who painted the drawing on the cover of this book-keep shining your light! Lastly this work would not have been possible without my parents, Charles T. Westcott and Catherine F. Westcott. Thank you for doing the very best job you could teaching me discipline, persistence, strength, and faith.

Contents

From The Darkness

Into The Light

From The Darkness

First Memories

I remember Howdy Doody on the small
TV in the dark 1950's living room in Wheaton,
Maryland and the single bed in the little
bedroom, being frightened of something
under the bed, or maybe on it, and Santa
Claus sightings by my brother who insisted
he saw him in the night sky Christmas Eve
when I was six, and the song from summer
camp *found a peanut, found a peanut, found
a peanut just now,* how sad the song seemed
to me then, and walking to church
and summer camp on Viers Mill Road, finding
treasures by the roadside for my secret box—
a marble, a trinket, a piece of jewelry.
I recall chocolate milk and not ever sleeping
at naptime in kindergarten. I loved
Tarzan and Pinky Lee, not multiplication
tables. I recall the attention
my toddler sister got when she broke
her glasses, and cutting my hand
in the dining room, a scar remains.
I don't remember my parents much—
if I didn't have pictures, I wouldn't
know that they existed at all.

Affirmation: I am a unique and blessed child of God.

In one sense, I raised myself, though not successfully at first. This led me to a life in which I sought ways to parent myself, to create joy, love, and happiness, as well as to seek healthy friends and relationships. My childhood propelled me to search out personal and spiritual growth experiences to attain higher levels of spiritual health. I do not regret this childhood because it allowed me to grow into a strong, resilient person. I was able to overcome a great deal of adversity and learn many life lessons.

The Lake Camp

I think of all the muddy bottoms
of lakes like the one near
my Grandmother's camp outside Troy,
New York. I remember the linoleum floors,
the musty smells of wicker and rollaway
beds. I seem to recall getting tangled
in kelp in the lake where I learned
to swim, the rowboat that took us far
out and my fear of the black snake
on the path to my aunt's cabin.
I can taste the blackberries by the roadside
we picked pricking our fingers
for that tart fruit and black smudge
on our hands and tongue. When I remember
the smells of pine, the crickets chirping
and the shouts of a dozen towheaded Irish
cousins, I see my mother's sweet enigmatic
smile, and realize that it was not just me
who was happiest those summers at the lake cabin.
My mother, absent her traveling husband,
was a whole different person.

Affirmation: I draw on the inner strength
and power I receive from God within.

I did have a happy childhood if I focus on
the good things like the lake camp outside
Troy, New York, which I shared with my
siblings, aunts and uncles, and cousins
for many summers. I first experienced
the joy of nature at Reichards Lake. I am
grateful for the many happy times and
the kindness of my aunts and uncles, who
still watch over me now from the beyond.

My Father's Cane

When I had no words, I listened to the rain,
to the crystal silence between the pages.
I could feel the cadence of my father's cane.

When I had no meter, I was not quite sane.
I looked for joy in trying to assuage
the memory of the cadence of my father's cane.

When I had no rhythm, I walked the lanes,
placed words on pages, a sauntering sage.
I sang to the cadence of my father's cane.

When I had no image, prosody was my bane.
I borrowed from Neruda: he was my gauge.
When I had no words, I listened to the rain.

When I had no lyrics, I let images reign
like the one of the heron standing on an edge
with one foot tapping like my father's cane.

I sat at the table to the right of pain,
to the left of father, away from his rage.
When I had no words, I listened to the rain,
and wrote the cadence of my father's cane.

Affirmation: I am happy and peaceful in the present moment. The past cannot hurt me.

To start writing is to begin an internal journey into who you are, what your feelings are, and what doubts, fears, and values drive you. Poetry for me became almost a necessity, a way of putting powerful emotions into concrete form, a way of channeling creative energy. Ultimately, writing became a survival tool. This poem deals with ways to survive. It stresses that writing can become a vehicle for not only the expression of difficult emotions and suffering but also a way of rising above it.

On Reading an Old Poem

Taking out the boxes to sort
and toss again, I recalled
memories of your quiet tears falling
on the kitchen floor, ashtray
on the counter like an urn, my resolve
to leave fueled by smoke and drink,
your marriage bed rife with ghosts
of former wives and me,
adrift in the haze. While I sunk
listless, lighting candles to
my Irish mother who was no longer
there to rescue me from a marriage-less love,
your twin daughters slept upstairs
in their dormer rooms. Confused and lost
under a pall, my hand began the slow crawl
back to the blank page.

Affirmation: I feel the love and comfort around me of those who are no longer here.

This is a poem of grieving in the present and anticipatory grieving of the end of an alcoholic relationship. I was stuck in a depression mixed with bereavement and trying to rise above it by writing. Sometimes it is necessary to just grieve, but it is always good to realize when to put the past behind and live life again. I can look back and see how being in this particular relationship kept me cemented in sorrow longer than necessary. I grieved my mother's death for a long time, but now happily communicate with her through mediums.

Fallen Evergreen

Needled by disease and regret,
I am reminded of a slanted evergreen.
Punished with longing for the husky bark
of your words, the bare roots of your sad
spirit, we have been felled by forces
too twisted for words in the forest
of sorrow. You gave me rings
of promise dropped like pine cones
onto a bed of barbed needles.
I cut our tree down in the woods
of lost childhood dreams.
As I lean into your memory, my heart
is darkened with the tar of your drinking
and scarred by your marriage to someone else.

Affirmation: I use relationships as a
way of expanding my awareness.

This poem is an extended metaphor
about a four-year alcoholic relationship
that I had. The tree of the relationship
was diseased and gnarled, but I kept
expecting it to grow back and become
healthy. By definition, one cannot have
a healthy relationship if alcoholism
(non-recovery) is involved. It took me
a long time to realize that. Al Anon
helped me see how toxic the relationship
was, but unfortunately that was
after the relationship was over.

Alcoholic Cardiomyopathy Before Your Time

Your death is all around me.
Your withered body gulps
a last breath of love.
Your vessels constrict
the flow of heart blood
just as your feet swell up
like the bellies of green toads.
You have been worn down
too long, too long
to find a path to me.

Your death is all around me.
You sleep upright
wheezing and winded
on three stuffed pillows.
You tire knowing sweet sleep
will not bring bigger death just
yet. Your enlarged heart exhausts
what is left of your love, the left
ventricle failing only weeks
before the right.

Your death is all around me.
Your tangled heart,
thick with dye,
will struggle,
gasp and you,
eyes bulging,
will cease:
the final abandonment.

Affirmation: I choose a different
path today, a path of recovery.

The dictionary says that addiction is a
strong and harmful need to regularly have
something such as alcohol or do something
such as gamble. This poem does not
reflect what happened but what could
have happened to a former fiancé after
being diagnosed with cardiomyopathy
at a relatively young age. I found that
going through the grieving and emotional
process of what his death would be like
helped me see that the relationship
had no future, and I was able to release
him to his new girlfriend, who was the
ideal partner for him at that time.

Regale Us

Remember in the old days of Hollywood,
with Myrna Loy and Lauren Bacall,
Marlon Brando and Humphrey Bogart,
cigarettes and sherry,
when modesty was a virtue
and sex a scandal?

Remember how you and I
soaked up the suds
in overflowing baths,
kissed the telephone with whispers,
how life was a carnival
of smells like sweat and lather
and Shalimar perfume?
Remember how you devoured my body,
crooned like Bing Crosby,
danced like Fred Astaire?

Remember how you yelled like Ralph Cramden,
questioned the color of my lipstick,
left like Bogey and Bacall.
Remember your slick promises
of roses and brandy and a life
of love taking away the pain?
Remember how you slammed down
the telephone with shouts and curses,
how life was a circus of doubts
and drinking and empty wine bottles,
how you listened to the rhythm of your heart only.
I remember how it was.

Affirmation: I can walk down a path of
thriving relationships that fulfill me.

This is a poem about remembering,
remembering the pain disguised as
promise and false hope and the glitter
of romance, remembering so as not to
be drawn into future dealings with
the alcoholic or to engage in fantastic
thinking about any hope the relationship
might have. This poem is based on
a second alcoholic relationship I
had, which ended traumatically.

Who I Left

While sifting through old letters
and pictures, I recalled you fast asleep
at the writer's gala, slumped in your seat,
while a poet read clerihews. I thought
about the weeklong silences, your Sunday musings
about grown daughters while you ate salmon
in wine sauce, blue eyes drooping and clouded.
I remembered the barbells in the bedroom, barren
living room walls, half-finished bathrooms
and toilets lying askew. I considered the tattered
teddy bears and broken furniture, remnants
of your children. It seemed like another life
when I said goodbye to your growing belly
in a cold bedroom with empty mirrors,
you nodding off to nightly sports results,
remote in a weary hand, gently snoring.
I was grateful I left you racing down
Macarthur Boulevard in your old Volvo,
belly filled with melancholy and wine,
speeding toward an office piled high
with old papers and potential lawsuits.

Affirmation: Challenges give me opportunities
for recovery and learning life lessons.

I like the Al Anon slogan, "you can't control the wind but you can set your sails." Once this relationship ended, I vowed to be more discriminating and to only select healthy, non-addictive individuals as friends and lovers. This poem refers to an alcoholic relationship with someone in a position of power over people. In many ways, I found it difficult to believe that this person could behave in ways he did, and I was in denial about the true nature of the relationship and his alcoholism The poem helped me remember that I could just say no, not engage with the person any longer, and that the false hope he offered would always be just fantasy, destined to fail.

Water Castles

Fantasies begin on unicorn wings,
glide like fish to silver seas,
rise like dolphins with a winning
smile, then spatter like rainbows
on a deep blue sky. Illusions drag
at the anchor of hope, tug at hearts
splintered like a glass on coral,
bitter as seaweed. Fantasies drop
swiftly into a roiled sea, sinking
sadly to the sand. What's left
whirls in the murky depths
with goblin sharks, vampire
squid, and dull-eyed salmon,
until the last shred of tattered
attempts plummet them
to the bottom.

Affirmation: I am worthy of being
happy, joyous and free right now.

Fantasy is defined as something that
arises from the imagination that
is removed from reality. This poem
describes how often I got caught up in
the fantasy of how things could be better
if the person just got recovery, could
see my point, would open up, improve
and so on, then life would be better for
both of us. In a sense, letting go of these
fantasies was the first step in taking
control of my life. It was another process
of letting go in order to move forward.

The Swimmer

Storms rose up on raging seas,
bitter as inky squid,
filled with barracuda men
with pointy snouts and fishy eyes.
I let those denizens wound me,
already washed to shore
like a beached whale.
What propelled me to swim
against that dark tide year
after year? Entering the next
wave, I rode its crest, the same
wave that knocked me down time
and again, the same bruising tide.
What drove this swimmer's dash:
the hope of a swim with angelfish,
a long float above the fray?

Affirmation: I do not dwell on the past,
but live in the present moment.

This poem represents the struggle I experienced to rid myself of demons, to step up to a more spiritual and enlightened life, to surround myself with happy, healthy individuals who are kind and who inspire and motivate me to become a better person. The tools for rising above the struggle were at my disposal, but I did not choose to use them at that time. Spiritual growth comes in layers and stages, and I accept that this was where I was at the time.

The Last Time I Saw Him

He was walking toward security
at Dulles airport.
He left like a jaunty jockey
about to start a race.
It was halfway between seasons,
the grey sky stayed dry
and paralyzed with moisture
building up inside. Later
the maple would drop
its leaves one by one,
each red leaf a letting go,
each yellow leaf hurt
as it hit the ground.

The weather was overcast
in the bleak way Washington
weather can be. The first week
was a foggy blur. I flushed
my body pervaded with a kind
of poison, detoxed my soul
with bubble baths and long
languid massages. I overcooked
a winter stew and dumped
the vegetables and meat
in the disposal, heard thunder
at a distance.

Later the rains came, alternating
between deluge and sprinkles.
In time, the dull drone of daily duties
replaced the lows, and the slow
undulation of a lake's movement
filled me.

Affirmation: I fill the void with God's
love and move on with joy.

This poem was written as an exercise
given in a class at the Omega Institute
in Rhinebeck, New York. The idea was
to write a poem without any emotion
explicitly expressed, and to get at the
emotion by other means. It is clear that
this describes the end of a relationship,
one of the several and last alcoholic
relationships I had. I also believed that
it was useful to grieve this relationship
before moving on. I grieved for what I felt
was the right amount of time for me to let
go of the past and move toward the future.

Anger

Is there a gift in thrusting
my fist into rough bark,
my hand worn and tired
while a sad tree drips leaves,
branches falling in disarray
across the hard brown ground?
Does yelling as loud as thunder
erase the hurt beneath the pain?
The raw sewage of my anger
seeps into the green earth,
poisoning with its fumes and stench.
I want to release my anger, breath
by breath, in and out, so that divine
energy dissipates it into thin air.

Affirmation: I am free when I forgive myself and others. I release all feelings that are negative and do not serve me.

I included this poem because although it is based on a negative emotion, I realized that all emotions are fleeting and that the faster I release them, the more space is freed up for joy and happiness. Today, I feel anger rarely, though it is a normal part of life after loss or disappointment. It's when the anger is not dissipated, or forgiveness does not enter into the equation, that the anger problem rears its ugly head. Now that I'm learning more about what anger can do to the body, and I'm coming into the last third of my life, I don't want to damage my body further by "wasted" time and energy spent being angry. This poem illustrates letting go of anger, and changing the energy.

Chest Pain

Once the pain lifted
off my chest like a hot air
balloon tilting toward heaven,
I vowed to release what
I could not use
like those Good Will items
piling up in my closet,
collecting the dust
of centuries of toxic
molecules, resting sadly
on the floor.
Could I also let go
of old anger and new
resentments collecting
in every corner of the house?
If only I could reduce
them to ashes, sweep
the lot off the balcony,
the heaviness would never
return, and I'd have a clean home.

Affirmation: I let go and let God.

I discovered that symptoms of anxiety and panic can mimic those of a heart attack. This has happened to me twice, once when I took an asthma medication and the other time after a difficult personal experience. In both cases, my heart was normal. It showed me how powerful thoughts were. The more I feared hospitalization, the harder my heart beat and the more my chest hurt. Only verification with medical tests convinced me my heart was fine.

Prayer for Letting Go

I felt helpless as a baby bird.
I wanted spring to hurry
its pace with daffodils and blossoms,
to speed its edge into summer
so work and cold could vanish
from a world that a sparrow could love.
But false hope caused me to stumble again
like a blind bird learning to fly.
My obsessive mind cried to the wind:
save me from corrosive thoughts polluting
the soil around barren trees.
Forgive me for presumption,
for wanting to halt the cold air,
the rain-drenched ground,
to have every moment in the passing
hours bend to my will.
My final wish: to be cradled in Your Arms,
soothing my emptiness with Your Light.

Affirmation: I say goodbye to things in my life that are blocking my spiritual growth, I allow life to happen with no expectations.

This poem shows the process of trying to let go, the awareness that I was not ready to do so and the ultimate lesson of turning the process over to God. In the grand scheme of things, I wished things would go the way I wanted rather than letting things flow. I wanted to control the outcome. Being in God's arms symbolizes surrender to peace, to calmness, to the flow.

Deluge in Rhinebeck, New York

Trees hide their beauty
from my blurred vision
as rain from branches
pinpricks my hatless scalp.
I wade through coursing puddles,
orphan grief from a mother's
passing buried. The sky—
a boxer's punch--flattens me.
Finally, in the drizzly dampness,
I look up at leaves, glistening
green plates, their random drops
becoming hopeful rain-lights
twinkling against the vast wetness.

Affirmation: I accept peace and joy into my heart. I accept myself unconditionally.

This poem was written at another retreat at Omega Institute in Rhinebeck and most of the week was drenched in rain. Writing this poem helped me to realize I was still grieving and I needed to let go into hope for the future and the beauty of the glistening leaves as a beacon. I am much healthier than I was in my early years when I had multiple cases of pneumonia, much sadness, and lingering grief. Once that grief was worked through, I was ready to begin a new chapter. Once my heart became lighter, my body became healthier.

Small Stone

It sat at the edge
of my heart, cold and hard,
lodged there permanently,
it seemed, as my cat shriveled
to bones and scruffy fur,
my tears gushing like a faucet.
I saw in my mind's eye her body
on the table, my final goodbye.
She had nine lives
and I wanted all of them.
For now, the stone broke away,
leaving me an intact heart,
and one more life for her.

Affirmation: I grieve my losses fully.

Washington Irving said there was "sacredness in tears. They are the messengers of overwhelming grief, of deep contrition, and of unspeakable love." My cat, Sarah, passed away on October 22, 2013. I grieved for her for a long time, and then I began to see that there was life beyond the presence of my furry friend. I planted butterfly bushes, saw Monarchs chase me in my yard, and felt her presence in each butterfly. She came to me through mediums, gave me advice and I let her go into the great beyond to run and play in a young healthy body. Oh, how I loved you, Sarah.

Another Life

I taste the wet kiss
of the Springer Spaniel,
drink my writer's cup
of café latte and praise
this one-sentence morning,
accept its gift of trees
replete with rain that drips off
soft leaves like a trickling faucet,
mint-fresh water still dribbling
and splashing onto the green grass
from thunderstorms, and I wonder
when I will start another sentence,
another life.

Affirmation: I am a unique and beloved expression of God. I can begin again at any time.

This poem arose from an exercise to write a one sentence poem. It seems in many of these poems that I have been waiting for my soul mate, but maybe it is just a search for God (but in human form). In a sense, there is nothing to wait for, nothing to do except start the life I want, be the life I want, and live the life I want. It is just that simple.

Not Lamium
(with apologies to Louise Gluck)

This is how you live with a broken heart.
As I do, living in corners with dust motes
and bits of paper dragged around by cats,
smidgens of lifeless material hiding just below
the surface or flotsam with its twiggy green legs,
reminding me that the lake is not pure, nor my heart,
as it once was when the priest leaned down
and said "you are the spitting image
of Grace Kelly."

This is how you live: silence, the cat scratching
along the wood floor, the fan whirring, the air
stale as summer, slightly moving eddies of breeze,
a heart beating somewhere, maybe drumming
into an early afterlife, a better version of life,
after you fail this one.

This is not how you live: dinner at five,
reading until bedtime, maybe an evening walk
with a mate along a flower strewn path
or forest floor, ferns green beside a brook,
the dog tripping along beside us.

This is how you live with an empty heart.
A step, then another step, until the calm
breath of hope picks up your tired body
and you try again.

Affirmation: Nothing endures, neither
good nor bad, so I will bask in the love of
God and surrender to the flow of life.

This poem is another example of my wish
to allow life to happen day by day, and
to get through the day until I make it
into joy and happiness when my body
is once again energized. In a sense, it
is "fake it until you make it"—what
the 12 step programs recommend. In
addition, I remember Lesson 293 of ACIM:
"All fear is past and only love is here.

Dear Melancholy,

Sometimes you creep up on me,
other times you are a snake,
coiling and uncoiling, black
and mysterious. I thought
you died last summer but in November,
you rose again just after Sarah died.
At first you consumed me, a kind of demonic
possession. I thought it was grief
over the passing of a beloved furry friend,
but you lingered through a tough January,
rain and cold and little outdoor life—
trips postponed, accumulating bad karma
and no prosperity. I tried to banish you
with bright light, dancing the night away,
but still you clung to me like a toddler
pulling at my leg, throwing a tantrum.
Hearing song lyrics like "I am a Rock, I am an Island,"
I decided to cry anyway, wanted to tell you
to go away. Instead I let you be, wrote
sad poems and eventually you disappeared
like invisible ink, this letter the only
memory of my melancholy.

Signed,

Affirmation: I am not my depression.
I am loved just as I am.

The quote "Although this night brings darkness to the spirit, it does so in order to illumine it and give it light" was written in the 15th century by St. John of the Cross. When I went through these dark periods, a friend validated that my depression was acceptable and ok. It also helped me to read Thomas Moore's book **Care of the Soul**, which indicates that depression is simply a state of being and not bad in itself, and I began to see that maybe it was part of God's plan. I could just be with the depression until it lifted.

I realized the lessons to be learned and what direction I needed to take my life. In addition, I became much lighter in spirit.

Wanting

I want a butterfly to land
on the bush in the back yard,
after it has been reborn
from a caterpillar.
I crave electric touch torching
my body, a heart fluttering
like a schoolgirl,
a smile wide across my face,
a hand reaching out across the universe,
feelings to flatten me, a giant wave
washing me under, whirling out
of control. I yearn to right
myself, and know it is real.
I want the moon to glow on
our faces together in biting cold
or chilly wind and clear skies
with sunshine warming our bones
after a long walk. I long for a sunset
in violets and reds proclaiming,
"It is good."

Affirmation: Today I will be grateful for small things.

The proverb and song lyric, "You can't always get what you want" is appropriate here. So is the Buddhist belief that suffering arises when we become attached to those things we do not have. For example, if we want a new house and become attached to that want and it does not manifest, we suffer. In a sense, this poem is a visualization of the life I want, knowing that at some point, I will get it. I pray for what I want and assume it will materialize. I visualize and dream of what I wish my life to be like, and in time it will happen, but I must let go of the outcome first.

The Lover Who Can't Let Go

I see the ocean shift
to winter's veil.
My sadness hovers
above the haze.
The skyline menaces
like sleet. I fear
I will never see you
again. Ships sail by,
flocks of black birds
scatter to mere memory
like thoughts of you
vanishing in billowy clouds.
I'm like a papery
old moth, worn down by bitter
words. I try to unpin
my hold on you and let
you go into the vast north
like a blue balloon
that rises to clouds
and vaporizes.

Affirmation: My strength lies in letting go,
not holding on. I let go and let God.

I used to hold on to the idea that a
relationship must last, to the false
hope that it would improve, that an
alcoholic would recover just by my
wishing it, until I learned that such
holding on can be a form of suffering
or a form of denial. I was also holding
on to memories of the good times, which
prevented me from moving on.

Cloudy with a Chance of Sun

Pallor-grey skies hide majestic rays
of sun, cast shadows on the land,
sap the energy of joy, mask
the love shine of God's eyes.
My heart mirrors these skies, waits
for the illumination of spirit in flesh,
the high bright light of love,
the kind hands of sunbeams warming,
the soft touch of understanding,
the soothe of summer showers,
the heat of luminous light
of God's sun when you appear.

Affirmation: My life is perfect just as it is.

This is another yearning or wanting poem. As already mentioned, the Buddhist teaching is that wanting is not desirable because attachment to anything causes suffering. I have had the experience of wanting something too much, and this wanting did not result in positive outcomes. This poem also expresses my belief that love is God, and God is all around us and within us.

Lies I Tell Myself

Today I will tell no lies.
I start the day with Truth,
look out at the magnolia
and see God in the green
swaying branches, angels
in birdseed to feed the blue
jays, harbingers of spring.
When I see butterflies not yet
butterflies, I will not lie
and say I am happy. When
I view the green outside
my window, the slice of blue sky,
the round arc of sun
on the branches, I will not lie
and say I am content. When
I am hungry for the breeze
to caress me, the bottlebrush
to protect me, and the hot
beating sun to warm my bones,
I cannot lie and say that is all I want.

Affirmation: I am valued and appreciated as a child of God, no matter how I am feeling.

This poem is an attempt to be honest about the fact that it is hard for me to be positive at all times. I sometimes feel that I am not in a state of Buddhist emptiness, Unity positivity, or lack of wanting, that in fact there are things that I do want. In the meantime, I take as gifts those things in nature, while absolute contentment remains elusive.

Recipe for Grieving

Pour a tincture of tears into
a glass bowl, fill to the brim,
then water the mums with half
the remains. Add myrrh
for mourning to give an ancient
texture, combining the tears
of all the heartbroken from centuries
past, then water the garden.
Find a half cup of regrets, toss
them in, then haul the water
from your overflowing eyes.

I scrap the recipe.
I want just one more day
with the soft furry body,
her morning squeak for food
at the bedroom door, me pulling
up the covers, the eager lapping
of Fancy Feast or Newman's Salmon,
the hop up to the chair to be brushed,
and the stroll to the lanai
to watch the birds, to smell
the fresh Florida breeze, to gaze
at the sea green bushes.
There is no recipe for acceptance.

Affirmation: I move on from grief with hope and joy.

Rumi tells us "Don't grieve, anything you lose comes around in another form." This is again a poem written during the time when my cat was dying. It was difficult for me because she was with me almost 14 years as a kind of soulmate. I had to make the decision to end her life, and it was the hardest one I have ever had to make. In the end, I celebrated the many gifts she gave me. It also helped to adopt two cats.

Wild Summer

I swivel into wildness,
have no quarrel with the speckled fawn.
The shaft of sunlight through the trees
chases away my funk. I gather in a group
hug with poets, we smudge our fingers
with s'mores and peanut butter and jelly,
gaze at the cerulean sea.

Sunlight splatters through the window
of the cabin, the sultry air of July catapults
me into summer's past. The branches reach
up to touch the sky and a lowly bumblebee buzzes
below. I walk with Emily Dickenson
through the woods, hear the choir of birds
and rustle of leaves this Sunday. I remember
when my heart was completely open.

Affirmation: I live with an open heart.

I began to see the wild joy that nature brought me, to get perspective on how I closed my heart as a result of the alcoholic relationships, and this did not allow room for love to enter my life. I needed to get bold about reframing my life, using animals and nature as guides.

Into The Light

Blue Snow

I

I confess that a kiss, a kiss beneath
the blue-black trees would be wet
in the soft blue-tinted snow.
I would rather kiss in the splash
of sparkling water, water blue as eyes,
on a serenely endless empty beach.

II

I wait for the cold beauty of snow
to melt my ache for summer.
The heat pumps out roaring air
in the cabin, while outside the blue snow
wants to melt into spring flowers
and carry the feet of kayakers
to the green-gray rivers filled
with fish and great blue heron.

III

I want to warm up to the chilly snow,
stark in its emptiness, blanketing
the future green shoots of spring,
now hibernating for a season.
The grass doesn't mind it's cold.
But I want four-leaf clovers and daisies,
blackberry bushes and apple trees,
wine and cheese near gurgling brooks,
to stretch out my legs
after a long ride and curl up
with strong arms and a soft heart.

Affirmation: Despite what is outside
of me, I am happy inside.

A friend asked me to write this poem
about a winter of heavy Canadian
snow. The background to the picture
was blue which propelled me to write
about blue snow. I realized that there
are good things in even the worst
weather, and I can choose which
"weather" I choose to live in.

Night

Pulls its shades on the beating sun,
protects from visibility like disappearing ink.
The night dresses in long black gowns.
Lamp posts shine on the beauty of shadowed bushes.
Night's stars: God's eyes on the world,
the moon His lighthouse keeper, letting
all corners of the globe be bathed
in reflective glow. Night trumpets
rest, rustling leaves usher mystery.
I love the night: it creeps up on you
like a child's game, everything
is possible. Ride it to its end
at the dull dawn light of nothingness,
or hide from it under covers
and eyeshades like clouds masking
the stars. Embrace the night
like a new born baby.

Affirmation: I am grateful for another day of God's grace and enthusiastically accept my good in the future.

Night is my favorite time. There is something magical in the moon, the stars, and the inky blackness outside the door. There is something eternal and infinite in the night sky.

Letting Go

is the song of stars tumbling
from black sky backdrop to rocks,
splintered on foggy mountains,
falling in a mad rush through thicket
and brush, sparks shooting out like
points of light, sinking through grey
bush, yellow flowers dotting the landscape
all the way to the sea's abyss, rolling
to rocks where waves, white in their fury,
wash over the shattered remains, cleanse
the bruises blue with hurt, drop further
onto waves away from the stones,
the hard edges, to the pure calm flow
of the Pacific seas, the eternal rocking
in the womb of God, the back and forth
cradle of life held within the sea's arms,
the single soothing serenity of green water,
washing away all the creases and tears
from centuries of wounds and slights
into the final undertow of release,
the to and fro of letting go.

Affirmation: I let go of what does not
serve me. I embrace joy and love.

This is a poem which arose out of an
exercise in a workshop at Esalen at Big
Sur. The poem seemed to tumble out of
me like the rocks tumbling to the seas.
Life is always a process of letting go, since
change happens all the time around us
and to us. As the Course in Miracles states
"to be born again is to let the past go."
It is in acceptance that we find peace.

Haiku in Big Sur

Shimmering ripples
like watery fireflies
sparkle at the cliff.

Grey undulating waves
shimmy in the sun,
show off for the sky.

Mountain feet planted
on the ocean's edge
remain unmoved by mankind.

Smashing wave bodies
against the cliff
bare their white bellies.

Naked nymphs in baths
near blue-white froth
ask nothing of the sea.

Butterfly, flutter free,
rising high to the eucalyptus:
nothing can hold you.

Oh, butterfly with broken wing:
feed on sweet nectar.
my heart bleeds.

Affirmation: I will feed on the sweet nectar of life.

This follows the butterfly theme and was written at Esalen where thousands of Monarch and other butterflies flew around us and on the bushes and trees all day during the writing retreat. It was a spectacular sight and I was impelled to write haiku about these butterflies.

A Rainy Day at the Beach

The rain falls on Madeira Beach
and I am in nature, the gulls swooping
to catch the grouper, the wind lashing
against the dock, the waves thrashing
onto the pier. Rolling clouds approach
ominously and lightning strikes
faster than an eye blinks.
The flashes never reach me,
they are always in the distance
like my mortality. Someday
I'll lie in a bed and earthly existence
will narrow, but that time is not now.

Affirmation: I will enjoy the moment and find pleasure in each day with no expectations.

John Ruskin has a wonderful quote: "Sunshine is delicious; rain is refreshing, wind braces us up, snow is exhilarating; there is really no such thing as bad weather, only different kinds of good weather." I knew I was beginning to recover when I made the best of a rainy day at the beach when the purpose of the trip was to lie in the sun and swim in the Gulf, and we had driven 3 hours in a bus to do so. However, we found the best fresh fish in a little hole in the wall restaurant, made new friends, laughed at the Tee shirt sayings in the shops that remained open, and passed a perfectly pleasant day. Sunshine would come again.

Self-Song

My song the sound of a butterfly's
flutter like the faint echoes of a bell.
I walk into the Rhinebeck woods,
a white butterfly encircles me,
flits to the grass, lands on bottlebrush.
She closes her wings, hunched in upon herself,
waiting. Just as quickly she darts up
and around until out of sight.

I ache for this butterfly,
like for my long dead mother.
I imagine her as a silent hello
from the beyond. Sadness passes.
I saunter out in summer's dusk
like a cat swaying on its haunches.
The baby blue sky swings into a muted
orange and red sunset. Further along
the path, a rabbit gives a doleful
stare, serene yet knowing. Faint sprinkles
drop onto the grass, glinting like fireflies.
I prepare to flutter on earth.

Affirmation: My joy radiates through my
heart and shines out to the world.

Butterflies are a passion of mine and
represent to me the spirit of past loved
ones. When my beloved cat died, I saw
many butterflies daily. I have come to
take great joy in the butterfly and rejoice
when one appears in my back yard. I
wish to flutter on earth like a butterfly—
hopeful, exuberant, joyous and free.

Angelfish

I always knew I was a fish,
my birth perched on the edge of Pisces,
water soothing me with its cool
enveloping embrace. Sometimes I dive down
deep just to see the lemon yellow kelp,
the slight pink coral like pincers,
brain coral infusing me with memories
of past loves. But I'd choose to be an angelfish, not
a grey fish. I'd draw a crowd with my blues,
more dazzling than the skies, without a hint
of white. I'd parade back and forth in my splendid
colors, never stopping to think about the bones
in my belly, I'd hear no sound of bells or music,
just the silence of the seas and other fish rushing past.

Affirmation: I open my heart to love and am
blessed with joy, peace and harmony.

I had fun writing this poem and it
again shows how happy, serene and calm
I feel in the water. When I am scuba
diving, I am almost in a meditative
state, and sometimes have had close to
a spiritual experience when diving.

Butterflies in Me

I have a butterfly in me fluttering high
to the eucalyptus. Nothing can hold me
as I swing upon the air, free to choose
the purple Tower of Flames or Pride
of Madeira bush to feed upon, free to fly
separate or alone.

I have a butterfly in me with a broken
wing. I am not any less beautiful
than my mates. I feed on liquid sweetness,
until I can't. Slowed down, I observe
others frenetically racing to a better bush.
I meditate on what is in front of me,
give thanks for the sun and flowers
and fellow travelers along the way.

But I am also that traveling monarch,
going great distances to seek out sweeter
nectar, hovering in my orange-black
beauty. What bliss to watch the Monterrey
Cypress sway in the breeze, the eucalyptus
stand watch over the garden, the mountain
at a distance allowing me to elevate above
the lowly bush, to seek higher ground.

Affirmation: All fear is past and only love is here.

This is another poem written at Big Sur. It was the first time I observed pairs of butterflies circling each other in the air, and I could rejoice in their freedom and exuberance in a gorgeous setting beside the Pacific Ocean. Usually butterflies alight on a bush at ground level but these Monarchs sought trees higher up. Seeking higher ground became a metaphor for greater spirituality.

Absence

Sunlight streaked through glass and I was free
to lazily stretch as on a bed of mums,
while somewhere far away on the high seas
in languid days of sun you could succumb
to shafts of light that beamed on waves and laughter.
Your absence an empty pond, a buried seed
thrust into dark and lustful soil just watered
to lie in shade and dark until there's fruit.
If I held your hand soft and slightly warm,
if l laid my head upon your brawny chest,
I would end the mulling in my mind, forlorn.
If only thoughts of you were laid to rest -
without the visits to empty pools again
until you return to me from where you've been.

Affirmation: I am able to enjoy life
even if my partner is absent.

This sonnet was written while attending
the Johns Hopkins writing program. I
was in the early stages of a relationship
and the poem showed me that the person
was important to me. His absence was
an opportunity to write a poem about
my feelings of missing him. By focusing
on the absence, I attempted to capture
longing and some sadness, but also a
kind of freedom in the emptiness.

The Reincarnated Mushroom

The mushroom shed wings
after its fifth lifetime,
retaining a beige color, slightly
speckled, growing long limber limbs
to remember its Creator. It reached up
to worship the ceiling above
dotted with white clouds drifting across
the morning sky. It had nothing to think
about but its being, no past or future.
If someone marred its perfect flesh,
the mushroom smiled and stood tall amid
the high grass of summer, often basking
in the sweet drench of rain plopping
on a round head. It was happy
in its perfection, surrounded
by disparate creations: the smooth stone,
the thick blade of green grass
and its welcome neighbor, the large
oak tree offering shade and afternoon naps.
Hidden from the summer blast of a mighty sun,
this mushroom is content.

Affirmation: I accept myself completely
and love myself unconditionally.

This poem arose out of a Writer's Retreat
at Omega Institute when the class was
asked to go out in nature and write what
they saw outside the door in the woods
of Rhinebeck, New York. In writing the
poem, I realized that each thing in nature
was true to itself, accepting of its state
and appearance and ultimate demise. I
began to love the little mushroom, flaws
and all, and realized that was what
God intended for all His creatures.

Dream

With life ahead, I'll go to sea again.
I'd like to cruise to Corsica this year
if just to curl my toes into the sand,
to feel my legs relax in fleeting waves,
to furl my hair like sails into the wind.
I'd like to touch the brightly glinting shells,
to watch the surf careen to rocks and froth,
the ocean tides recede and swell each day
so surf could fling my sighs to darkest night.

I'd like to par a hole with a ball that flies,
avoid the sand and water around the green,
to be with friends on a blue-skied sun-filled day
who praise my game when balls lift off like birds,
who comfort me when I fail to hit the mark.
I love the greening hills and heron cries,
the whirring cart that tumbles over grass,
the soaring ball allowing me to play
a game that gives me joy in every way.

With past behind, I'll traverse the trails ahead,
the pebbly paths with ponds and palms nearby.
I'll feel the wind upon my cheeks at noon,
the sunbeam's warmth just lighting up my face,
a kayak drifting in rivers short and wide.
I'll dip and glide like slithery fish at play.
My arms will slide through bluish pools again,
as sadness sinks below the setting sun.

Affirmations: I exhibit joy and exuberance
by thinking happy thoughts.
I thank God for the joys of nature.

This poem was written as an exercise in writing in iambic pentameter. I added two stanzas to it when I moved to Florida to reflect my love of golf and kayaking. After escaping cold and wintry climates, I began to notice clouds, heron, sunsets and other joys not available to northern urban dwellers during certain seasons. A recurrent theme is that when I am out in nature, I am most at peace and happiest. I am glad I have chosen to spend winters in Florida.

Thoughts

I care about the clouds darkening
in the distance, whether black skies
lay ahead, the fact that butterflies
run from wind and scarce flowers,
that the sun has made only
brief appearances this week,
and I feel like I'm back North.

But today I have no peevish thoughts.
A Monarch caterpillar forms
a J on the leaf in my back yard,
the glare of blue sky returns,
and five yellow butterflies
herald the spirit of my late cat.
Later, the night rings crisp and pure
and possibilities stream endlessly.
I can live with just the sun
and trees and stars and moon,
and the transformation of nature
outside my door.

Affirmation: Every day of my life is positive, happy, and full of sunshine.

This is again a truthful poem, one that shows how my mood can change with the weather. However, when I count my blessings and see the display of nature and new life outside my door, my feelings shift.

Costa Rica, Blue Spirit

I am breathless, breathless
for you to reside within
the empty spaces of a heart
  too far
from love, the kind of love that
  swims
with dolphins, sings with
  hummingbirds
as they flit to ferns from trees
with manic happiness, the kind
  that sinks
into the lush grass of the soul,
in paradise that is not yet
paradise where butterflies
lead you to sides of stream soft
with moss near the woods of
  acceptance.

I want a poem.
I stride down to the white
  waved sea,
walk along the tide pools
between black lava rocks,
watch the minnows.
I step from rock to rock
all the way to the sea
in low tide. A blue crab

defends itself from my extended
toe, scurries across the water.
A motionless Spoonbill guards
the bay, stares with wary eyes,
moving only its head. Terns and
  gulls
dive for breakfast in long
  swoops
then splat—a fish. I watch sea
  snails
scrawling circular trails
in the sand, drawing patterns
like an ancient mosaic.

It is a perfect morning,
sun not too high,
locals selling their pots,
a new friend holds my hand
in my mind. Mountains rise
in the distance What is
on the other side?
I etch in my memory
these moments, hoping
they can be retrieved later,
taken off the shelf
like a porcelain horse.

Affirmation: I am a radiant being,
enjoying life to the fullest.

This poem was written at Blue Spirit Retreat Center in Costa Rica at a week-long retreat sponsored by Omega Institute in January of 2013. Writing was part of the retreat and I found inspiration in the ocean, the minnows, and the Spoonbill and what was happening on a moment to moment basis. Just like with all happy memories, I wanted to preserve them, mull them over in my mind, to brighten a day in the future which may not be as lighthearted.

I am

a Monarch butterfly flying over the Pride
of Madeira bush for a drop of nectar

I am the hard black rock in the sea,
white waves crashing over me
in the morning

I am the condor plume feeling
the fierce air of Pacific coasts

I am the softened stones near shore,
the evening waves lapping gently beside me

I am the eyes of a deer
not hunted, gazing on the face
of a man of peace

I am the star you see first thing
at night if you look closely

I am the rain that pelts
muddy mountains, the sun-joy
in the morning

I am not Alpha and Omega
but I exist now and into the distant
future,

and you will hear me
in my words.

Affirmation: I am one with the presence of God, and divine life renews every cell of my body.

In this poem, I become one with the sea and deer and rocks and butterflies, acknowledge that there is only one Creator of all, and set forth my life's purpose of writing my spiritual journey.

Walk to Melody Lane

I first notice them when the streetlights
don't shine, just beyond the heat lightning
and silhouettes of white clouds, those pinpricks
of light sprinkled in the summer sky like glitter
on an eye. The stars, my keepers, lead
me away from myself, promise in their twinkling
madness a vaster life than the flatness
of declining years and a good cry
when beauty and love overwhelm, remind me
of a walk on slithery grass with bare feet
after a rain, the soft engulfment of water
on my body. I look up at nature's naked display,
make plans to time travel to the most distant star.

Affirmation: I am protected and safe
in the light of God at all times.

I love the saying by Sai Baba: "Observe the stars, millions of them, twinkling in the night sky, all with the message of Unity, part of the very nature of God." This poem originated from an exercise to write what came up when taking a walk. Since night is my favorite time, and I feel a strong spiritual connection to nature, this poem sprang up automatically and was one of the few poems that was easily written.

Atlantis of the Soul

Should I take the staircase down
or the one going up, stone steps rising
in a crescendo of swirls and turns
into the ascending air? Is it not wiser
to move down an ever-declining spiral
to depths not plumbed?

As I walk into the waiting green-blue waters,
I see the faint outline of stairs,
step up to my neck in water,
toss on fins and gills, breathe deeply.
I gasp as my head dips under,
blow the air out in a quick puff
and descend further.

Spotted fish and turtles
swim by me as I glimpse
the silhouette of a city.
I hear nothing, no whirring
of auto engines or crowing of hawks.
I hike deeper, leave behind
earthly ways, rest in the womb of water.

Shedding my skin, I await a new world,
not a mirror image of the one beneath sky.
I have found my Atlantis of the soul,
am greeted as if newly arrived in paradise.
My Christian sins and Buddhist karma
and godless deeds are washed away
in the waters of forgiveness.

Affirmation: I forgive daily and am healed and renewed.

Reinhold Niebuhr said that "forgiveness is the final form of love." I think that is a beautiful way to express how important forgiveness is. This poem arose out of an exercise in a class at Omega Institute with the instructions to begin a story and see where it took you. This poem involves water, for its purity, for its essential nature, for its giving of life. The idea of being washed in forgiveness is very appealing, almost a baptism or cleansing of the spirit. I believe that we must constantly release and let go of what does not serve us, to leave room for the flowers of our soul to bloom. As Lesson 297 of The Course teaches: "Forgiveness is the only gift I give."

Walking Meditation at Esalen

I walk alone on the wooden deck,
gazing at the peach-red sunset
over the Pacific, admire
the Monterrey fir branches
arranged for a picture against
a backdrop of sheer cliffs
and green-fogged mountains.
I hear the whoosh of waves crashing
to rocks, and realize I will walk alone
to my grave, a culmination of walks
over a lifetime, strolls at midnight
or early morning, hikes on paths
or streets. Walking with intention
makes even a walk to the mailbox
an adventure, blue birds flitting
across the trees, a rabbit darting
under bushes, clouds a downy white
in the distance. The walking meditation
still lingers, not like the forgotten walks,
those mundane sleepwalking strolls,
those tired heavy hikes of a life
not wholly lived.

Affirmation: I find peace and creativity in the silence.

Voltaire says that "meditation is the
dissolution of thoughts in Eternal
awareness or Pure consciousness without
objectification, knowing without
thinking, merging finitude in infinity."
I attended a writing and meditation
retreat at Esalen, and it was a gloriously
productive and healing time. The
walking meditation exercise was one
I had not tried before and helped me
see details and patterns in the trees,
flowers, mountains, sea. The retreat
workshop was located high on the cliff
overlooking the Pacific Ocean at Big Sur
and was the inspiration for this poem.

Our Body is One with Water

We are the basin containing the water
of all the oceans, all the rivers
whose tributaries lead to fields
and mountains. Hot springs live
in our bellies, pumping healing energy,
and rain taps lightly on our chests,
opening our hearts. We are the Pacific Ocean
on a stormy day, rise up in power to crash hard
against the rocks, gleeful crowds
admiring us. We are the Jordan River,
have baked in the heat of centuries,
our sparkling water tumbling over rocks,
glinting in the sun of spring. Cargo ships
to fecd the masses travel over us,
and we give pleasure to boaters zipping
over our soft bodies. We hold angelfish
and damselfish in our arms so divers
can gaze on them. We are the vessel,
we are the container.

Affirmation: I am one with God and all creation.

Jules Verne states that "the sea is everything. . .the sea is only a receptacle for all the prodigious, supernatural things that exist inside it. It is only movement and love; it is the living infinite." This poem to me is a reflection not only of that statement but also of The Course in Miracles teaching that we are all connected to one another. In a way, we are connected like ice, water and steam in that they are all different but are really the same thing. When I think of myself swimming in a pool or ocean, I can feel that oneness with nature and as a result oneness with God and all beings.

Angel's View of the Seasons

Spring

Clouds of tears drench
the greening land
and mountains below.
Angels roam over fields and farms,
crops that feed the earth,
over areas of checkered squares,
meadows and emerald trees.

Summer

tames the lions of ice and hail.
As moon flirts fitfully with sky,
the land returns to green and gold.
Angels alight on heaven's trees,
pull the shades on sighs.

Fall

blows in fluttering waves
of yellow and orange.
Angels float to peaks of leaves
that drop and crunch beneath
the feet of children. Spirits
perch on heaven's gates.

Winter

Clouds and fluffed beds
of white billow shed goose down
for the Beloved. Snowy mountains
cast shadows on whitening plains.
Angels slip on wings to fly.

Affirmation: I honor my soul's essence, as I let my light shine brightly. I allow my angels to guide and inspire me.

"To everything there is a season and a time to every purpose under heaven." Eccl 3:1-8. This poem was written in response to an assignment in a class led by the wonderful poet and teacher Reuben Jackson. To me, every season has a purpose, and though I much prefer summer and spring for the frequent and longer day light, there must be dark (winter) in order to come into the light.

Musing near Nags Head Beach at Dusk

I step over stones and shells,
dip my feet into the water's
cold tang while snowy egrets,
white as clouds, arch their necks.

I watch the flock of brown pelicans
skim the swells in their southward
trek, gauge their larger purpose
as they fly.

The froth of white caps
flows onto the beach, less furious
than in yesterday's storm.

I wonder if the silver fish,
deflated on the gritty sand,
willingly give up their tiny bodies.

The ocean teaches ceaseless
pleasures, movement toward
no end in particular,

and patience—the sand crab
poking his head out of a hole
in low tide, curious, then
retreating.

I wonder and wander the beach.

Affirmation: I am open to the guidance
of Spirit. I honor the wisdom of my soul
and trust in the guidance I am given.

This poem was written while spending
a week in Nags Head, North Carolina.
Even though the trip was somewhat
challenging, I decided to enjoy the
ocean and to write a poem about
the pleasures I found there. I began
thinking of larger cosmic questions
and forgot my petty concerns. I became
one with the birds and fish and sky,
and in a sense my spirit was reborn.

Meditation

I want to go deep into the
  sphere
buzzing with the energy of love
like bumblebees on honey,
  creamy
words whispering "cara mia."
I want to be surrounded
by love beings picking me up
from bruises and schoolyard
  slights.
After meditation, I want to be
  paralyzed
like a statue, unable to enter
the real world, clinging to that
bit of heaven I was allowed.

II

I meditate with an open heart
whose soul has traversed the
  globe
many times like Amelia
  Earhart.
I receive you while dressed in
  an apron
with my apple pie cooking in
  the oven,

smells of childhood wafting into
  the room,
drawing you to me, allowing
  good
to enter even without the secret
passcode, after faith tiptoes in
on soft slippers. I bathe in the
  light
of my ancestors, fling open the
  final
gates to the castle.

III

Meditation: a way of clearing
  the mind,
clearing the chatter of monkeys
  jumping
from branch to branch over the
  river
lazy with alligators and heron,
meandering to the next corner,
letting the wind blow
its soft waves east, then west
in ripples wide as a wood duck's
wings, traveling far from its
  origin,
the mind of meditation.

Affirmation: The peace of God lives
in the quiet of my heart.

I love the thought of T.S. Eliot that
we should "be still and wait without
thought." In many ways, it summarizes
what my journey should look like,
waiting without thought, waiting
and meditating, even if there is not a
desired outcome immediately. I have
found meditation to be incredibly
healing, and have incorporated it into
my daily practice. Whenever I forget, I
become unbalanced in my life. When I
devote more time to meditation, I feel
refreshed for the entire day or night.

Ode to the Moment

Dawdling moments
fetch parcels of surprise—
each new moment a lesson:
patience, how fear closes,
how time is no one's servant.
I borrow bits of time, restoring
them in meditation like a wise
god. This moment cries out for rainbows
to eclipse the gray. While a Siamese cat
rubs against my leg, another plane
arrives in Paris. Now I'm slowed
down to the sound of muted traffic
in late summer's dusk, crickets
buzzing outside in tall oaks.
I see my life made up
of moments, the past
moments smaller and
smaller like a
Russian
doll.

Affirmation: I let the past go and look forward
to the future. I trust in God within.

"Do not dwell in the past, do not dream
of the future, concentrate the mind
on the present moment," is a quote
from Buddha. I find I'm most in the
moment when meditating or writing
or making love. There is a quality of
timeless time. This poem, written after
a meditation/writing group session, was
an ode to that tiny bit of time called
a second when so much can happen.
These moments in the past do get smaller
and smaller as I let go of the past.

Mind of Winter

Life has delivered dark winters
of traffic jams and icy roads and the trap
of four walls without the smell of pine.

I like the pure essence of snow,
the innocence of children sledding down
snowy hills with leggings and big mittens,
a cup of hot chocolate at home.

My mind of winter is ice blue snow,
packed hard on the sad ground, waiting
to burst forth into the song of spring

with asters and yellow roses and raspberries
red on the lips, apples tart on the tongue,
four leaf clovers crossing their green fingers
for a short winter.

Now I experience the butterfly rising
to the nectar, the long hot days
of languor on a boat in cool rivers.

Affirmation: I can weather the challenges life puts before me. I accept the comfort and strength of God.

This is another peon to spring and better weather, something that brightens my spirit. The more I learn to let go of perfect "weather" and accept what is in front of me in all respects, the happier I am.

My Place of Meditation

Grey and white streaks of clouds
paint the morning sky on my way
to the sea, the moist air smells
of recent rain and fresh washed trees.
The ocean spreads out below the hill,
crashing into eternity. Briny salt
on my lips, I walk up to the waves
as they smash and foam, wait for
the effervescent froth, then dip
an ankle, a leg into the cold tang.
Swimming in the azure ocean, I feel crisp
and clear as water, a sparkling drink.
I glitter like the glinting sun
on the seas. I want to always feast
on my contentment, the water's soft touch,
its gentle rocking of my body, and stay
forever in the water's embrace.

Affirmation: I shall remain as calm and soft as water.

Water is always healing for me so it is no surprise that when asked to conceive of a lovely place to return to in meditation, it involved water. There is a kind of cleansing tranquility that I associate with water, a calmness and serenity I experience only in meditation. There is a kind of womb-like safety I feel with the ocean.

Gratitude

It is a day ripe for gratitude,
a time to bypass desire, to cherish
blessings blowing like linen
on a line in a spring breeze.

It is a day ripe for miracles
to grow brighter and more
magnificent, to obscure the pale
petals of denial and regret.

It is a day ripe for freedom
and gratitude for the will to ascend
out of darkness and discontent
to the blue world above.

It is a day ripe for the glory
of asters, the sunbeam of forgiveness,
the love light at sunset.

It is a day for gratitude to rise up,
swoon at the full moon, praise God.

Affirmation: I take time to be grateful for something as simple as the blue sky. I am grateful for an abundant and full life.

I have found that since I have begun a daily gratitude list, that abundance multiples. If I take time to be grateful, even if the day is not going that well, I find that I'm much happier and see things in a different light. The twelve step programs are right in that cultivating an "attitude of gratitude" is a remedy for most of what might come up in life.

Metamorphosis

Shrunken to a shrink-wrapped body, sinking
into the sand, shrouded in fear
like the pallid shadow
of a hunted animal hiding
in holes, perhaps a hedgehog,
prickly, pushed down
to a nub of self,
stick-thin, fading
into grayish fog,
the sun behind clouds,
a petal not opened.
Scrunching in seats,
she swallowed words whole,
pain shot through sciatic nerves.
Swilling filtered water,
jean-clad, she swung sideways
to spirituality, sunk in the sadness
of saints. A naked tree stands
against the landscape, waiting to bud.

She now walks with the mystical
flower of prayer, power
in luminous flesh, slinks
with the grace of a panther,
desiring nothing. She soars,
a sea gull over grasslands
where sympathy simmers
in creek beds circled
with fern and moss,
cirrus clouds embellishing
the sky. She is a sparrow
needing nothing, a thorny
rose in bloom.

Affirmation: I am grateful for the positive things still to come my way. I am at peace. I am whole and healthy in mind, body and spirit. I go forward to achieve my purpose.

I like this poem as the last poem in the book as it summarizes my journey and mentions most of the spiritual tools I have used: prayer, meditation, forgiveness, nature, and the power of God within. Although technically I have less appreciation for this particular poem, I chose it as the last poem because it summarizes my path from darkness to light. As lesson 75 of ACIM states: The light has come.

Poems Previously Published

"Fallen Evergreen" in **The Federal Poet**, Vol. LXX, No. 2, Fall 2012

"Regale Us" in **The Great American Poetry Show**, 2004.

"Chest Pain" in **Loch Raven Review**, Vol. Viii, No. 2, Summer 2012

"Rickards Lake" in **Broadkill Review**, Vol. 6, No. 3, May/June 2012

"My Father's Cane" in **The Federal Poet**, Vol. LXIII, No. 2, Fall 2010

"Ode to the Moment" in **The Federal Poet**, Vol. LXIX, No 1, Fall 2011

"Musing near Nags Head Beach" in **Guwahatian emagazine**, Vol. 1, Issue 12

References

A Course in Miracles (ACIM), Foundation for Inner Peace, Viking, Penguin Books, 1996.

"Sai Baba." **BrainyQuote.com**. Xplore Inc., 2014. 27 December 2014. http://www.brainyquote.com/quotes/quotes/s/saibaba184101.html

"Buddha." **BrainyQuote.com**. Xplore Inc., 2014. 27 December 2014. http://www.brainyquote.com/quotes/quotes/b/buddha101052.html

T.S. Eliot, **The Four Quartets**, East Coker, 1940.

"Washington Irving." **BrainyQuote.com**. Xplore Inc., 2014. 21 December 2014. http://www.brainyquote.com/quotes/quotes/w/washington149294.html

St. John of the Cross, **Dark Night of the Soul**, Chapter IX, Book II

Thomas Moore, **Care of the Soul**, Harper Perennial, 1992

"Reinhold Niebuhr." **BrainyQuote.com**. Xplore Inc., 2014. 27 December 2014. http://www.brainyquote.com/quotes/quotes/r/reinholdni121403.html

"Rumi." **BrainyQuote.com**. Xplore Inc., 2014. 27 December 2014. http://www.brainyquote.com/quotes/quotes/r/rumi132950.html

"John Ruskin." **BrainyQuote.com**. Xplore Inc., 2014. 28 December 2014. http://www.brainyquote.com/quotes/quotes/j/johnruskin108460.html

The Holy Bible, The 21ˢᵗ Century King James Version®, copyright © 1994. Used by permission of Deuel Enterprises, Inc., Gary, SD 57237. All rights reserved.

Jules Verne, **Twenty Thousand Leagues under the Sea**, Pierre-Jules Hetzel, 1870.

"Voltaire." BrainyQuote.com. Xplore Inc., 2015. 6 January 2015. http://www.brainyquote.com/quotes/quotes/v/voltaire118531.html

Zhuangzi, **Butterfly as Companion: Meditations on the first Three Chapters of the Chuang-Tzu,** Kuang Ming Wu, 280 BC (approximately)

Biography

Mary L. Westcott began writing poetry 25 years ago and has been published in more than fifty five literary journals. She holds a doctorate in social psychology and an MA in Writing and is retired from the National Institutes of Health. She has been on a spiritual journey, including recovery from several alcoholic relationships. She lives in The Villages, Florida with Rocky Rio and Didi, her two rescue cats.

CPSIA information can be obtained
at www.ICGtesting.com
Printed in the USA
FSOW01n2337291116
27905FS